DARE TO FLY!

"They Shall Mount Up with Wings as Eagles"

Bill McClung

Author's Tranquility Press
ATLANTA, GEORGIA

Copyright © 2023 by Bill McClung

All rights reserved. No part of this publication may be reproduced, distributed or transmitted in any form or by any means, including photocopying, recording, or other electronic or mechanical methods, without the prior written permission of the publisher, except in the case of brief quotations embodied in critical reviews and certain other noncommercial uses permitted by copyright law. For permission requests, write to the publisher, addressed "Attention: Permissions Coordinator," at the address below.

Bill McClung /Author's Tranquility Press
3800 Camp Creek Parkway, SW building 1400-116, #1255
Atlanta, GA 30331
www.authorstranquilitypress.com

Ordering Information:
Quantity sales. Special discounts are available on quantity purchases by corporations, associations, and others. For details, contact the "Special Sales Department" at the address above.

Dare To Fly/Bill McClung
Library of Congress Control Number: 2024903959
Paperback: 978-1-959930-96-9
eBook: 978-1-959930-97-6

Contents

Introduction 1
Joshua and Caleb Mentality–"We can do it!" 5
Why do so many Christians live in Defeat? 9
God's Part—Our Part 21
Doing Good Works: Is it God's Will or Not? 29
Released from the Power of Sin 33
Romans 6: The 'set-free' Message 37
Wretched Man: Who Shall Deliver? 45
The Sin Problem and the Double Standard 49
Surviving the Storms 53
Spirit of Truth and Spirit of Error 55
Like a Roaring Lion 63
The Measure of Success or Failure is Love 67

Introduction

When I was thinking about writing *"Dare to Fly,"* I thought about Orville and Wilbur Wright and their daring quest to build and fly an airplane. They thought outside the box (that, in the minds of the majority of people, thought was impossible and couldn't be done). Only a few had a dream or ventured into the area of possibility.

The brothers, Orville and Wilbur, humble bicycle repairmen, ventured where few had dared venture. Both were dreamers at heart. Their dream of flight became a reality in 1903 when they became the first to experience powered flight. They did this despite the many voices of skepticism, negative disbelief, and sometimes even mockery.

Many Christians today approach their walk in Christ the same way. They surmise that there is no way they can take that daring step higher, of a closer walk with the Lord. There is a widespread belief that we are bound to our sins; therefore, it seems impossible to be overcomers in this life. Many are like turtles, scooting on their bellies as close to the ground as possible, barely making any headway in their Christian walks. There is very little growth accompanied by much defeat and sinfulness. Few see the possibility of flying with Christ on a higher plain.

My wife Shirley and I were pilots and owned our own airplane. We loved flying! The perspective of seeing things from above of God's magnificent creation that couldn't be seen at ground level was exhilarating beyond words! To fly at a higher level; To fly faster and further in a given time were also greatly appreciated benefits.

Our greatest enjoyment in our experience in flying, was sharing the wonder of flight with others. It was such a satisfaction in seeing others experience what we had. That's my desire in the sharing of this book. I desire and pray that *'Dare to Fly'* will produce inspiration for all of us to get spiritually airborne!

Some folks that we invited would not accept our invitations that we extended! They had doubts, being fearful and not understanding the physics of flight! They surmised that if, for some reason, the engine failed, that the plane would plummet to the ground immediately. They were afraid of heights. Their fears kept them from experiencing the joys of seeing things from different perspectives; that of flying higher, moving faster, and covering more territory in a shortened time.

A scripture comes to mind in **Isaiah 40:29-31** with **verse 31** being the ongoing theme of *'Dare to Fly'*: ***"He giveth power to the faint; and to them that have no might, he increaseth strength. Even the youths shall faint and be weary, and the young men shall utterly fall; But they that wait upon the Lord shall renew their strength;*** <u>***they shall mount up with wings as eagles;***</u> ***they shall run, and not be weary; and they shall walk and not faint."***

In the Bible, the apostle Paul saw beyond the ordinary, beyond the status quo, when he stated, ***"I press toward*** *the mark for the prize of the high calling of God in Christ Jesus."*

"*Dare to Fly,*" is an endeavor to inspire and give hope to Christians who desire to be overcomers, who desire to live victoriously in their Christian lives, and who have a longing to grow closer in their relationships with Jesus.

Newly born-again Christians start out as student pilots, learning from their teachers, exhorters and pastors, whose written manual is the Word of God, the Holy Spirit being the chief flight instructor.

My longing is that each one of us will see the great possibility of climbing one step higher. Oh, that we could step out of our comfort zones and into the glorious realm of flight experienced by that of an overcomer's life! It's not that it will be easy or free of difficulties, trials, and hardships. But the rewards far outweigh all of that.

The messages contained in this book came from many personal learning and unlearning experiences. In addition, this author is thankful to the Lord for the received insightful revelation from the Holy Spirit. Ultimately, it was through much reading from the flight manual, the Word of God, that spawned the inspiration for the writing of this book and the messages contained therein.

Joshua and Caleb Mentality— *"We can do it!"*

Jesus said, Luke 18:8 NLT: *"When the Son of Man returns, how many will he find on earth who have faith?"* I believe what he was implying was that faith would be a rare commodity. It was in Jesus' day also. He was often quoted as saying, *"Oh, you of little faith."*

I was thinking of how much opposition those who express strong words of faith experience. They are not only experienced from our generation but that of the Biblical generations as well.

Jesus was rejected by his own people. After all, to them, he was only the son of a poor carpenter. The Bible says that amongst his own hometown folks, he could perform few miracles because of their unbelief.

Then there were Joshua and Caleb. What a lesson there is to be learned in their lives and attitudes! Moses was instructed by the Lord to send spies to spy out the land of Canaan. Twelve supposedly top-notch rulers were sent out to do the spying.

Ten of them came back with an evil report full of fear and pessimism. **Numbers 13:31 says,** *"We can't go up against them! They are stronger than we are! The land we traveled through and explored will devour anyone who goes to live there. All the people we saw were huge.*

We even saw giants there. Next to them we felt like grasshoppers."

Only two spies, Joshua and Caleb, had a wonderful and positive report. *"Let's go at once to take the land. We can certainly conquer it." And if the Lord is pleased with us, he will bring us safely into that land and give it to us. Do not rebel against the Lord, and don't be afraid of the people of the land. They have no protection, but the Lord is with us! Don't be afraid of them! But the whole community began to talk about stoning Joshua and Caleb. Then the glorious presence of the Lord appeared to all the Israelites at the Tabernacle. And the Lord said to Moses, How long will these <u>people treat me with contempt?</u> Will they never believe me, even after all the miraculous signs I have done among them? None of those who have treated me with contempt will ever see it. <u>But my servant Caleb has a different attitude than the others have.</u> He has remained loyal to me, so I will bring him into the land he explored."*

Joshua and Caleb were the only two out of the twelve, who believed that God could and would take them into the land of promise. Like the persecution that David and Jesus received, they too received the same—treated almost like they were enemies.

When I've shared the possibility of going into our promised lands, I've quite honestly been baffled and taken back by the opposition and animosity. When the very mention of possessing that land where there's peace, joy, happiness, and close fellowship and communion with Jesus, our general—I get this look of, *"Who do you think you are? You're only human. You'll fail just like us!"*

What they fail to realize is that yes, I would fail, except we Christians have the very God of the universe with us and in us. He will give us the victory through the power of the Holy Spirit! We are well able!

When we share about victory or when we exhort about going in and possessing the land, we are speaking about territory that is in our adversary, the Devil's control of envy, jealousy, hypocrisy, hate, impatience, worry, and all the works of the flesh.

We are to go into and possess the land of love, joy, peace, longsuffering, patience, and the fruits of the spirit. That is the land flowing with milk and honey! It is ours for the taking!

I want to have that same attitude and spirit that Joshua, Caleb, David, and Jesus had. *"We can do it! For our God is able!"*

I have been so blessed over my life with a few living examples of such men and women of real faith. My grandmother was such an example. Every time there was a problem or trial she would say, *"Our God is on the throne! Let's go to prayer!"* She gave God thanks and glory <u>for everything</u>! She had a child-like unshakeable faith with no doubts about God's Word or his promises–all of them! She led many to salvation through her word testimony, testimony of a life of victory, and the testimony of her rock-solid faith. She was so sold out to God; her whole life taken up with pleasing the Lord and doing his will. But like others that have strong, unshakeable and unwavering faith, she suffered persecution from those that didn't understand her faith and exuberance. Her overwhelming and genuine joy radiated from her life. Those in close communion with the Lord loved her and loved being around her! Her life and faith were so contagious! She lived in Omaha, Nebraska, and I in Oregon. I wished I could have been around her more! What little time I did have with her, left an unforgettable impression and was forever embedded in my life.

I find there is such a need for much more faith; even in my own life. I have such a hunger to be around and witness those who will rise up against the tide of unbelief and have a Joshua and Caleb-like spirit! We will need it in these last days more than ever before. Real genuine faith is indeed rare and precious!

I am thrilled when I hear of people getting saved, being set free from alcoholism, pornography, overeating, impatience, judgmentalness, bitterness, worry, self-righteousness, and many other addictions and sins. What a joy! What victory! What conquering of the enemy of men and womens' souls!

What a land of milk and honey is the inheritance to those who say and believe, *"We can do it!"* **"With Jesus as our captain, leading us into battle; How can we lose? If only we have faith in him and trust him totally!"**

Why do so many Christians live in Defeat?

I've heard and witnessed much defeat and negativism concerning the possibility of Christians being able to live God-pleasing lives in wonderful, triumphant victory. And yet I see the scriptures saturated with words of triumph and victory available for the believers! I am of the opinion that God has given us all the tools and resources necessary for his children to live victorious, fruitful lives through Jesus.

I believe that our Heavenly Father is unhappy when, after being our Provider in these areas, for us his children, not to use the tools and resources he has made available to us. I believe we also **underestimate** the delivering power of the Holy Ghost in our lives that gives us the ability to overcome the evil one.

Many preach, teach, and share that victory in Jesus is absolutely not possible! Or they will speak as though God will do and perform everything for them. That, according to Scripture, is simply not true! While God is in our hearts and in our beings, he requires us to yield our bodily members as instruments of righteousness to accomplish his will and to be in obedience to him. That is **our responsibility**. The Word of God is full of instructions and commands for you and I to do and perform.

God's responsibility is to supply us with all the strength and power we need to accomplish these goals. But the doing, performing, and obedience burden falls on us. God and us (co-workers together with him) make it possible to bring about victory over our sins, weaknesses, and inadequacies. It's through the power and authority of the Holy Spirit within us that makes victory possible.

What should be the Christian's motivations for overcoming sin anyways? First and foremost is that we love and want to please Jesus with all of our hearts.

Secondly, we desire to be all that God has envisioned us to be in growing more and more into his image.

The third reason: Obviously, sin causes harm, heartache and damage to us spiritually. It can also affect us physically as consequence of specific sins such as worry and bitterness. Those damages can affect not only the individual who is guilty of these sins but also those he or she is in contact with in daily life.

Let me clarify and be perfectly clear. This message is not presenting a perfect utopia where Christians never ever make mistakes or never fall into the trappings of sin.

Nobody is ever completely free from unknown sins, failures or shortcomings. We can, however, triumph over those sins we understand to be sins. If we do sin, we have the privilege of coming to Jesus for the forgiveness of sins we know to be sins. Also, there are those sins that we never knew to be sins before; but God through the Holy Spirit's illumination reveals them to us. We can take those to the foot of the cross as well for cleansing and forgiveness.

There are different avenues the Lord uses to illuminate unknown areas of sin in us: The Holy Spirit through the preaching and teaching of the Word—Revelation through reading the Bible—the Holy Spirit's revelation speaking and convicting us individually. Also, God uses our time of sharing fellowship with each other in the Body of Christ, as we speak into one another's lives, to illuminate those yet unlearned, unknown, and dark areas we don't understand in our individual lives yet. This is all a growing experience. We stumble, fall, repent, and rise up many times in the embryo stages of our Christian walks. **But we ought not to remain babies our entire Christian lives!** We can walk in victory as overcomers with God's divine power working in us.

We can only work on those areas of our lives and be obedient to what we know to be wrong and unpleasing to our Lord. So, yes; There are areas that will on a continual basis, be enlightened and revealed to us. Then and only then can we do our part in being rid of even those unknown sins and shortcomings. This painful but delivering process will take place in the life of the believer as long as we have breath. The Bible says, *"–and if we sin, we have an advocate with the Father."* Praise be to Jesus for that. Where would we be without his forgiveness? Where would we be without his grace to cover our unknown areas of failures, unaware weaknesses and failures, and un-illuminated sins in our lives.

II Tim. 3:15-17 (KJV) says, *vs. 15 "And that from a child thou hast known the holy scriptures which are able to make thee wise unto salvation through faith which is in Christ Jesus."*

To be saved <u>from</u> sin and become more like Jesus, requires being in the Word. We need its teaching and wisdom, combined with faith in that which we read. Many are defeated because they do not know what the Bible speaks concerning the power and authority that is at their disposal, in defeating sins, and ultimately the Evil One.

II Tim. 3:16 (KJV) says, ***"All scripture is given by inspiration of God, and is profitable for doctrine, for reproof for correction, for instruction in righteousness."***

Notice the word *'all'.* Many believers read or concentrate on small portions of scripture. Therefore, they suffer malnutrition in their walks with the Lord. They lack many spiritual nutrients needed for normal Christian growth. They stagnate in their spiritual growth. They live as Christian babies that never move ahead nor mature in their relationship with Jesus.

Another reason for Christians experiencing defeat is because of misleading and inadequate teaching regarding victory through the power of the Holy Spirit. Numerous modern-day teachers and preachers of the Gospel are messed up in their doctrine (theology). They steer away from any teachings found in the Bible regarding *reproof*–regarding *correction*–and regarding *instruction in righteousness* (that lifestyle that is well-pleasing to our Lord and Savior). Therefore they, as well as those under their tutelage and preaching, are spiritually sick and weak and remain in their sin bondages. Those same brothers and sisters are ill-prepared for what Satan throws at them on a daily basis. They are easy prey for him. We are no match for the devil if we are ill-equipped and ill-prepared.

We that share the Word of God have much responsibility as well as tremendous accountability. We have much to answer for. We must teach and preach the *full* gospel in all its purity, simplicity, and truth. Life and death are in the power of the tongue. And by our words we'll be justified, and by our words we'll be judged, the Bible says. If we share in such a way that causes people to keep on sinning and stumble in defeat; God will hold us accountable! We must love the truth at all risks and all costs. It may cost us, as teachers of the truth found in God's Word, to be rejected by well-intentioned brothers and sisters in the Lord. We could be misunderstood as being dogmatic, legalistic, and judgmental. But it's God's Word that each and every Christian shall ultimately be accountable to. The Bible really is the ultimate teacher. We teachers and preachers of the Gospel are just vehicles that God uses to share these trues. If people are offended, they may not know it; but they are offended at God's Holy Word–not just offended at the hoses that he chooses to use.

Ephesians 6:10-17 speaks of putting on the whole armor of God. The question is: Who is to do it? The answer: You and I are! <u>God will not do it for us!</u> Many wait and wait on God to perform everything while they sit back and do nothing! Then they wonder why they are still so bound to their sinful natures.

It very well could be that Satan defeats Christians because they do not put on the whole armor of God. Or if they attempt to; Their armor is incomplete. There are chinks and gaps in their armor. That is exactly the target area that Satan will tempt and attack you at–at your weakest area of vulnerability of protection or lack thereof.

Eph. 6:10 (KJV) "Finally my brethren, be strong in the Lord, and in the power of his might."

Many do not understand that there is a need for total dependence on the Lord's power if they are to experience victory over known sins in their lives. They try to overcome sin on their own power and strength. They try and fail because they are missing the key ingredients: the power of the Holy Spirit and faith. We will fail every time we rely on our own strength to obtain victory over sin without God's help! In addition, victory is unobtainable if we do not read and in faith believe what God's Word has to say concerning victory and triumph over sin.

Another reason for defeat is that we fail to call out to the Lord in our time of need when we're being tempted. For many years, I was ill-prepared for what Satan and my flesh threw my way in regards to temptation. It was a constant cycle of <u>temptation</u>–<u>sin</u>–<u>repentance</u>. This vicious cycle of defeat repeated itself over and over again. I failed to realize that I could trust in the might and power of Jesus. I didn't understand that all I needed to do when I was tempted, was to call out to him for HELP! When I learned that principle—when I called for help when I was being tempted; God <u>always</u> answered my prayer. He never failed me, nor will he anyone who calls upon him. It is no sin to be tempted. Even Jesus was tempted, yet without sin. Sometimes in the heat of battle we forget to call upon Jesus. May God help us concerning our forgetfulness. He can help us grow in that area as well.

Eph. 6:11 (KJV) "Put on the whole armour of God, that ye may be able to stand against the wiles of the devil."

Eph. 6:12 (KJV) "For we wrestle not against flesh and blood, but against principalities, against powers, against the rulers of the darkness of this world, against spiritual wickedness in high places."

Many Christians do not understand the spiritual warfare that they are in. There is a need to understand who the enemy is and what he's up to. They are armorless and without spiritual weapons! However, through Jesus, both are at our disposal. Besides the armor mentioned in **Eph. 6**, the Bible also says in **II Cor. 10:4** *"The weapons of our warfare are not carnal, but mighty through God to the pulling down of strongholds."* We must be aware that there are powers and principalities in the spiritual realm that are bent on our defeat, incapacitation, failure, and our utter destruction.

I Peter 5:8 & 9 (KJV) says, *"Be sober, be vigilant; because your adversary the devil, as a roaring lion, walketh about, seeking whom he may devour: Whom resist stedfast in the faith, knowing that the same afflictions are accomplished in your brethren that are in the world."*

One reason that Christians get kicked around by Satan and live defeated lives is because they are asleep–spiritually speaking. They are drunken with activity and cares of this life. There is a lack of vigilance. Because of that tendency, God's children need to be wide awake and aware of what is going on at all times. There's a need for understanding when they are being attacked. Satan's attacks do not catch off-guard those that are of this mindset.

Eph. 6:13-17 (KJV) "Wherefore take unto you the whole armour of God, that ye may be able to withstand in the evil day, and having done all to stand, Stand therefore, having your loins girt about with truth, and having on the breastplate of righteousness; And your feet shod with the preparation of the gospel of peace; Above all, taking the shield of faith, wherewith ye shall be able to quench all the fiery darts of the wicked. And take the helmet of salvation, and the sword of the Spirit which is the word of God:"

A big percentage of Christians are only equipped with partial or incomplete truth. They have only been equipped with part of their armor. Only limited instructions on battle plans are in hand.

Another key ingredient lacking is the shield of faith. Many brothers and sisters are full of so much unbelief. This great lack of faith is partly due to bad teaching, partly to unclear understanding, and sometimes a total lack of hunger for the undefiled truth found in God's Word. The Bible is full of victorious teaching and instruction. Yet many do not believe what is written. Their carnal minds tell them that it is impossible to do anything pleasing to the Father—that it is impossible to keep from obeying their sinful natures–that we are slaves to the works of the flesh (contrary to what is taught in scripture). It's no wonder Satan's darts get to them so easily! It's no wonder they are sinning over and over the same sins, with little or no progress in their lives. It's no wonder the virtues and fruits of the Spirit are so lacking! It's no wonder there aren't more Godly examples that would cause the people of the world to desire to have what they have! If there's no deliverance from addictions and sins, if there's not something better for the world to look forward and up to; Why would they want what we have? If they are hopelessly in despair because of their deep bondage to sins and addictions and the damages it causes in their lives and those they are around; Why would they look to people who claim to be Christians for the answers and solutions if those Christians are in the same predicaments of defeat, bondage, and despair that they, as lost sinners, are captivated by?

Another reason Christians live defeated lives is because they are not willing to suffer in the flesh and take up their cross daily as the Bible speaks of. The Bible says, ***"They that have suffered in the flesh have ceased from sin."*** No suffering—then no ceasing from sin! It's a painful process when our flesh wants to do something that makes it satisfied and feel good, yet at the same moment, the spirit of God in the new man he has put within us is saying, "No!" To take up our cross daily is an unknown entity to many believers. The cross was a symbol of suffering and death. We are to suffer in our flesh and daily die to self–deny ourselves and say "no" to sin and "yes" to Jesus. To fight the good fight of faith–to take up our cross daily–to deny ourselves is painful. Armed with the mindset and attitude that suffering in the flesh is part of the territory as overcoming believers, we can experience joyous victory in our lives. Freedom brings great joy and peace!

When Israel was being attacked by Goliath and the Philistines, Saul and the armies of Israel were fearful with a total lack of faith in God's power to deliver them. They were paralyzed to even fight! They felt that they were surely going to be defeated! The enemy was too great! Goliath was too huge and strong for them! Many today approach their weaknesses and sins in the same way the Israelites did with their enemies.

But David—little David, the shepherd boy was full of child-like faith! May God give us the faith to slay the Goliaths (sins) in our lives. May we say to Satan as David did to Goliath, *"You come to me with a sword and spear; but I come to you in the name of the Lord of hosts, the God of the armies of Israel, whom thou defied. This day will the Lord deliver you into my hand and I will smite thee, and take thine head from thee."*

It's time we take the head off our enemy, the devil! It's time we become the victors and not the victims! It's time we become, as the scriptures say, *"more than conquerors in Christ Jesus."*

It's time we discard our masks of false humility in bragging about our sins and failures. That mindset only strengthens and encourages others to continue in their own sins. **James 5:16** mentions, *"Confess your sins to each other and pray for each other <u>so that you may be healed</u>."* The whole purpose and goal in confessing our faults and sins are so that we can be healed and set free. Do we truly want to be healed? Do we want to be unchained from the sins that bind us?

It's time we stop giving Satan glory for our defeats. It's time that Christians experience true victory in their lives. It's time for God to be glorified in personal testimonies of deliverance **from** sins and addictions! That's true humility! Children of God who are overcoming, realize and acknowledge that they could never ever accomplish anything victorious or perform the good works that Jesus has created them to do without the power of almighty God! But through Jesus, *"All things are possible to him that believeth."*

It's time that we not only have testimonies of God's healing power and of the wonderful things he has accomplished in and for us in our natural lives—but for his deliverance **from** evil and his setting us free **from** our sins and bondage as well.

There is victory in Jesus to all who, in faith believing, call upon him in their time of need. Victory belongs to those who are equipped with all their spiritual armor and weapons! To God be all the honor and glory for this great possibility and challenge!

God's Part — Our Part

There's a great effort on Satan's part to prevent God's people from experiencing victory over trials, temptations, and sins. I am hearing many preachers who teach that there needs to be no effort on our part—-no choices and decisions to be made— no actions to be taken by believers in overcoming sin and evil in their lives. They say that if we exercise faith alone, that the Holy Spirit will do all the work toward victory for us.

We need to be like the Bereans and see if this mentality and doctrine is correct. Why would the Bible tell us in **Col. 3:5** *to "mortify the deeds of the flesh?"* If there was nothing for us to do but have faith that the Holy Spirit would do it for us. Is there personal action for us to be taken, by an act of our will and by being obedient to the word *'mortify'*?

II Peter 1:5-8 (KJV) "add to your faith virtue; and to your virtue knowledge; And to knowledge temperance; and to temperance patience; and to patience godliness; And to godliness brotherly kindness; and to brotherly kindness charity. For if these things be in you and abound, they make you that ye shall neither be barren nor unfruitful in the knowledge of our Lord Jesus Christ."

Who does the <u>**adding**</u>? Who gives forth the work and effort to be in obedience to that scripture and command? I could go on and on concerning the countless instructions and commands God has given us in his word that is directed to the individual. We could put the word *'you'* in front of every one of them.

Eph. 6:11 (KJV) (You) *"put on the whole armour of God."*

Luke 9:23 (KJV) (You) *"take up your cross daily"*, (You) *"**deny yourself.**"*

Matt. 5:44 (KJV) (You) *"love your enemies"*, (You) *"**work out your salvation with fear and trembling.**"*

That certainly sounds like decision-making and action-taking to me!

If you solely put your faith in the Holy Spirit and trust that He will do it for you without any effort on your part; Victory will always elude you without your doing of the steps and actions God requires of you.

It is true however, that we absolutely must have faith and trust in the Holy Spirit! He gives us the power that we don't have in our own strength. However, God expects action on our part. He always has! And He always will! He expects us to decide to be obedient and do what's right in his sight. <u>That will always be our choice. He will not force us into obedience or righteousness. He will not do it for us!</u>

We need to, as the Bible says in **Hebrews 4:16** *"come boldly to the throne of grace in our time of need."* (times of temptations, trials, and tests). Genuine faith produces action and *conscientious* decision-making on our part.

The fruits of the Spirit only happen in our lives as we abide in the vine. That means that we exercise faith, have confidence in the Lord, and trust him as our sole source for victorious power.

If the fruits of the Spirit are only byproducts of being in the vine—Why does **2 Peter** tell us to *'add'* many of these fruits to our lives?

We see through God's instructions and commands that there is definitely something we can and are required to do if we are to have the fruits of the Spirit evident in us. They are to be desired, sought after, and put into practice.

It is clear, according to the Word of God, that we are co-laborers and partners together with Christ in our ***"working out our salvation with fear and trembling*** as it is ***God working in us to will and do of his good pleasure." (Phil. 2:12 & 13 (KJV))***

Our part is obvious in the first portion of that scripture. God's part is the last part of that verse.

II Cor. 6:1 says, ***"as God's partners, we beg you, not to accept this gift of God's kindness and then ignore it."***

I Cor. 3:9 states, ***"We are laborerers together with God."***

Phil. 2:12 & 13 Paul instructs us that <u>we</u> are the ones who must work out our salvation (the victorious life through Jesus). It is <u>us</u> who must move to action. It is <u>us</u> who must choose right from wrong. It is <u>us</u> who need to obey the commandments of the Lord. It is <u>us</u> who must put on the Lord Jesus Christ, put on his virtues and the fruits of the Spirit found in **2 Pet. 1:4-7**. They also agree with those found in **Gal. 5:22-25**. It is us, through the power of the Holy Spirit within us, to move in action (perform if you will) and put forth the effort. It is not an automatic thing, as though we are mere robotic creatures in which we have no say or control in life's situations, trials, tests, and temptations.

It is dangerous for us to put our minds into a state of neutrality. We absolutely need to put feet to our faith! *"Faith without works is dead."* is stated in the book of **James.**

It is equally dangerous and unbiblical to say that, "There is nothing we can do, and that "We must cease from working, performing or doing in the battle of life."

It is not right nor biblical to state that all we have to do is put our faith and trust in the Holy Spirit to automatically perform outside of our cooperation and participation. It's through obedience to the Word and following the promptings of the Holy Spirit. It's through the power that the Holy Spirit provides. We need to be totally dependent, having our confidence in and exercising our faith in God alone as our source of strength and power. We have a need to give up doing and trying to accomplish God's purposes and will on our own with willpower only. We have a need to understand just how weak we are without God's provided strength. Then, and only then can true victory be ours. Without Christ and his power, we can do nothing. But with his strengthening and with his empowerment, we can do, as **Phil. 4:13** so clearly illustrates, *"I can do all things through Christ which strengtheneth me."*

The Lord is in the process of refining and fine-tuning our way of thinking and use of words. This is especially the case when we are speaking about God's part and our part in our Christian walks.

Our words are weighty and of great importance. Words of extremes such as: ***Always, Never, Only, All of the time***, or ***None of the time***, are just a few radical words that come to mind. They can be dangerous and misleading.

We know that we can use words unconditionally and biblically correct in situations like, "God ***Always*** is truthful!" and "God will ***Never*** fail us." God will ***Never*** lie!" There is no problem with such extremes of wording if the Bible says so!

It becomes problematic when we use those words when they are actually untrue in and by themselves. They can be the source of much confusion and error.

For example: When it comes to God's part and our part in our purification and cleansing from sins; Many will believe and say, "*We can **never** cleanse ourselves or change our hearts. Only God can!*"

Really? Is that really true? The fact is that the Bible has many scriptures which speak concerning us <u>cleansing</u> and <u>purifying ourselves</u>.

I would emphasize that the Holy Spirit is very much in action in this process also. But, is there a part I am to play in my cleansing and purification process? The answer, according to the Word of God, is a resounding, *"Yes!"*

An example, which illustrates our part, is found in the verses that state, ***"Forgive others their trespasses. For if*** *you do not forgive others their trespasses; God will not forgive you."* Forgiving others is my part in the cleansing of myself equation. God's duty is cleansing us and our hearts at the same time we are performing our part.

Found below are scriptures that command us to cleanse and purify ourselves and are 100% true statements concerning doing our part in the purification and cleansing process:

II Cor. 7:1 (KJV) "Having threfore these promises, let us <u>cleanse</u> ourselves from all filthiness of the flesh."

James 4:8 (KJV) "<u>Cleanse</u> your hands ye sinners and <u>purify</u> your hearts ye double-minded."

II Tim. 2:21 (KJV) "If a man therefore <u>purge</u> himself from these, he shall be a vessel unto honor."

I John 3:3 (KJV) "And every man that has this hope in him <u>purifieth</u> himself, even as he is pure."

Our Heavenly Father has a major role in this cleansing purifying process and the scriptures below verify that:

Jer. 33:8 (KJV) "I will <u>cleanse</u> them from all sin."

Psalms 19:12 (KJV) "<u>cleanse</u> thou me from secret faults." (that which the Lord does)

I John 1:7 (KJV) "...and the blood of Jesus Christ his Son, <u>cleanseth</u> us from all sin."

Heb. 1:3 (KJV) "...when he had by himself <u>purged</u> our sins, set down on the right hand of the Majesty on high."

When we pray, we should ask God to cleanse, purge, purify, and forgive us of our sins. We also are wise to ask him if there is any part that we have in that process. *"Heavenly Father; What would you have me to do? Give me the strength and power through the Holy Spirit to do my part."*

So we understand through these scriptures that there is my part and there is God's part. The words ***Always***, ***Never***, and ***Only*** can muddy the waters of our understanding as to what we are responsible for and to do.

In **Phil. 2:13** where it mentions God's workings in me and to fully picture and understand that in my finite mind, and just how that all works, does and may always remain a mystery. It is like trying to fully comprehend, understand and have a vivid picture regarding the God-head and trinity and yet oneness. If we're truly honest, I think we'll only know some of these great mysteries in their complexity when we get to heaven.

A few things that we can know and understand regarding our roles and God's:

1- We are co-laborers together with Christ and have our part. He will work in and with us as partners; not in replacement of us.
2- God is working in and through us and by us in accomplishing what he wants to accomplish in our lives. But he will not do it without our cooperation, obedience, effort, and yes, even hard work!
3- We are totally dependent on the Holy Spirit for our help and grace in time of temptation, trials, and needs.
4- We are to exercise faith in God alone, not relying on our own strength.

5- Since it is He who is working in us and is our source of power, there is no room to glory or pride in oneself! We are mere vessels and instruments in his hands. ***"Without Christ, we can do nothing,"*** is clearly stated in the Bible.

I believe it is of vital importance to have a correct understanding of these powerful principles found in God's Word. It is so clear as to what our part is and what the Holy Spirit's duty is in obtaining and walking the victorious life that is made available to us.

To walk in the Spirit, doing our part, is the one step higher that we can take. Walking in these trues will create a closer sweet relationship with Jesus our Lord and Savior. At the same time, we'll triumph and grow more and more into the maturity that he has in store for us. The sky's the limit!

Doing Good Works: Is it God's Will or Not?

First of all, I want to be on record: that I believe we are saved only by the grace of God and his great love for us. We don't deserve it! We can't earn it in anything we do! Jesus paid for it entirely with his precious blood. That was the only price that could be paid that was valuable enough as an offering to his Father that could satisfy the payment for our sins. No amount of goodness or works on our part would or could qualify us for even the slightest of God's mercy, forgiveness, or love, let alone pay for our salvation! Our eternal salvation is only secured and bought for by the great sacrifice of Jesus precious blood and sacrifice of death on an old rugged cross.

That does not mean that we are exempt from doing good works; as many teach, preach, and believe. Nor does it imply that putting forth effort towards doing good works is a bad thing, as some suppose. The Bible says, ***we were created unto good works."*** It also states, ***"We will be judged by our works."*** Though our good works will never save us; Good works bring glory to God. Good works, produced through Jesus, are very precious to him. They are needful for us to pursue and do!

Many believers repent, are born-again, baptized, and attend church–some for many years. But these same Christians walk lives of defeat. They never grow in the Lord. They remain baby Christians–some thought they've known the Lord for a long, long time. A close relationship with Jesus is non-existent in their lives. Many are unaware of the great possibilities that children of God have at their disposal. They are unaware that Christians have the possibility of growing daily and of walking out a vibrant, victorious, exemplary life. Many don't realize that it's God's will and desire that they become molded into his image. There exists a lack of understanding that they can and should be growing in Christ's virtues and fruits of the spirit on a daily moment-by-moment basis.

The reason for the lack of understanding is because many believers do not get into the Word of God for themselves. They gullibly take teachers' and preachers' thoughts concerning these issues as truth—lock, stock, and barrel, so as to speak.

I can never emphasize enough; That it's because of Christ and the Holy Spirit's working in and through us, that we are given the power to do the impossible in our lives—using us as instruments in his hands, to do the things pleasing in his sight—and the things he requires of us.

Though our flesh is very weak; He is powerfully strong! He is our power source. He is the gasoline in our tanks. Without him, this vehicle will go nowhere! ***"All things are possible to him that believeth."*** the Bible states.

Another phrase that could <u>mislead</u> the believer is: ***"It's not about performance or a set of rules."*** Our salvation surely is not! But our pleasing the Lord, our growth in him, and our daily lives are!

However, our attitudes and motivations must not be like the Pharisees of wanting to be seen by men, to be flattered, to exalt self, or any other selfish motivations; We **do**, because we want to please Jesus. We **do** because we want to bless and build up others. When it comes right down to it; We **do** because we love Jesus so much, that we want to make him happy and pleased with us. We **do** because we love people so much, that we would even be willing to lay down our lives for them. The book of **James** exhorts us this way, *"Be doers of the Word, and not hearers only, deceiving ourselves."* It's all about relationship. Our **doing** God's will and purpose in our lives is only accomplished through having a personal close communication and relationship with Jesus on a continual basis.

God's commandments are not optional! Neither are his instructions and emphasis on good works optional! They're not mere suggestions that we can ignore or minimize in selfishness to please and gratify our flesh.

Another few thoughts: The Bible speaks about dead works. Those works produce pride, self-righteousness, and judgmentalism. It's works with selfish motives. They are works we do because of our own dreams, ambitions, and thoughts.

On the other hand, there is Christ's righteousness, worked out through us. That **set of** righteousness (good works) is orchestrated by the power and leading of the Holy Spirit in our lives.

Dead works displease the Lord. They are done through one's own efforts outside of the Holy Spirit. They are as wood hay and stubble and will burn up. They are, as the Bible puts it, *"are but filthy rags."* They are of no value in the eyes of a Holy God.

The righteousness produced by Christ, pleases our Heavenly Father. In addition; The righteousness that is from above is precious in his sight. This type produces life and good fruits in the believer. We must never mistake that type of righteousness as filthy rags! The righteousness that is from above is only accomplished through the power of the Holy Spirit in our lives; Why would we call that kind of righteousness *"filthy rags"?*

So yes; The truth of the matter is that good works are God's will for our lives. They're mandatory commodities. But they're also glorious, precious, and pleasing in his sight.

A few scriptures to read and ponder:

James 2:17 *"Faith without works is dead."*

Rev.20:12 & 13 *"judged according to works"*

John 14:12 *"and greater works shall he do, because I go to the Father."*

Titus 1:16 *"They profess that they know God; but in works they deny him, being abominable, and disobedient, and unto every good work reprobate."*

Jesus said, *"Why do you call me Lord, and <u>do</u> not the things I say?"*

Released from the Power of Sin

What the Church needs desperately and is so lacking these days is a real genuine move of FAITH in the Word of God–not a counterfeit faith–not an empty hollow faith–not a presumptuous faith–but a simple child-like faith that believes every word of God in the scriptures with no doubts or hesitations. It's better to put a passage we don't understand on a shelf until such time that God opens our eyes to its true meaning and revelation to us. It's better just to admit that *"I don't really understand this or that scripture just yet."*

Many Christians, because of their preconceived ideas or theology, try to explain away, misinterpret, or simply ignore parts of the Bible. They build up shells to the truth. The longer they do this, the thicker the barrier and shell become. Right interpretation and understanding certain scriptures will always elude them. Blindness and hardness sets in if they continue to harden their hearts to truth. Only through tender and open hearts can God deliver us so we can truly know truth and see through his eyes. May God transform our way of thinking and change us daily.

Matt. 7:24 says, *"Therefore whosoever heareth these sayings of mine, and <u>doeth</u> them, I will liken him unto a wise man, which built his house upon a rock. Vs. 25: "And the rain descended, and the floods came, and the winds blew, and beat upon that house; and it fell not: for it was founded upon a rock." Vs. 26: "And everyone that* *heareth these sayings of mine, and <u>doeth them not</u>, shall be likened unto a foolish man, which built his house upon the sand" Vs. 27: And the rain descended, and the floods came, and the winds blew, and beat upon that house; and it fell: and great was the fall of it."*

What Jesus was doing was equipping us with instructions of what it takes to stand victoriously. If we don't do what he tells us to do, we'll crash when the trials, temptations, or any other hardships come our way. In these last days, the rains and the floods are viciously battering Christians. The question is: *"Will my foundation fall or will it stand firm and secure."* It's all a matter of trust, faith, and obedience to Jesus. Without any or all of these (trust, faith, & obedience), our houses will not stand when the storms of life hit.

Many modern-day preachers and teachers are in error when they tell us that, "There is nothing we can do." "Jesus did it all." While it is true that Jesus did do it all; He has paved a new and living way under a new covenant. He lived a life that you and I can follow his footsteps and do it too! When he lived in a fleshly body just like ours, and overcame the evil one, and ultimately died on the cross; He not only did that for our forgiveness—but also he destroyed the power of sin in our lives. He did it to release us from sin's powerful stranglehold on the lives of his dear children. He did it to set us free and render sin power<u>less</u>. Sin shall no longer enslave or hold us captive if we trust in Jesus and the Holy Spirit. Read **Romans 8.**

Romans chapter 7 speaks much about the weakness of the flesh under the old covenant (without Christ's redemptive power and without the power of the Holy

Spirit). Paul explained what a wretched man that he was before Christ came with the solution that Paul mentions in **Rom. 8:3 & 4.** The whole victorious message in **Chapter 8** refers to the new covenant which Jesus authored and ushered in. It speaks about us walking in the Spirit and not in the flesh. It talks about being set free from our fleshly dictates as we trust in and have faith in what Jesus accomplished on the cross and in his life. It talks about being set free from the fear of being bound by failure and defeat as spoken in **Rom.8:15, 21, & 22** as was the case under the old law—as also is the case when we walk in the flesh and not the Spirit.

In **Romans 7** where Paul recognizes his wretched condition and being a slave to his old sinful nature, (doing the things he didn't want to do & not doing those good things he really wanted to do. The old law came as a horrifying revelation to him of his weaknesses and failures). He felt helpless until he realized there was a way out of his predicament. Jesus introduced a new covenant which paved the way for VICTORY over those former bondages. The law under the old covenant made Paul so aware of his helplessness and hopeless condition. **Romans** also tells us that it wasn't the law that caused him to do those evil things and not to perform the good in **Rom. 7:10-24.** It was the weakness of the flesh!

We desperately need power and strength from above. We will miserably fall short and fail without that power and strength. Jesus is the source of all our power and strength. Jesus lived the life well pleasing to the Father. He paved a new way for us, his beloved children, and followers of him. He did it in human flesh fashioned just like ours. He defeated Satan, on the same familiar territory that Satan had from the beginning harassed and held man in captivity and defeat. That territory was the FLESH with its crippling weakness.

Jesus didn't come to earth with his Divine body, but one like yours and mine. The Word says, "Jesus did it first! He came in flesh and blood so he could be our faithful high Priest. He overcame in a body of flesh and blood like ours so he could empathize with what you and I are being tempted with, and what we are going through. The Word encourages us to come to him in our time of need. That is so that he can supply all the grace and help to get us through our situations (temptations) victoriously. He already defeated Satan. He did it so you and I can do it too! (follow in his footsteps).

So, yes, we can overcome and be victorious over sin! We can grow more and more into the image of Jesus. We can, through the power of the Holy Spirit, walk in close relationship with Jesus, as we faithfully walk in obedience. We can overcome all that we understand and have knowledge of to be sin. We also can be sensitive and obedient to new revelations to weaknesses and sins residing within us, in which we have no knowledge of as being wrong as of yet. We can't overcome something we don't see yet. We are in a continual growing and learning process. It takes our entire lifetime of being sensitive and obedient to the Holy Spirit's promptings and conviction in our lives in rooting out those things that are displeasing to our Lord.

We can boldly say, *"I can do all things through Christ who strengthens me."* –at the same time in humbleness of mind, knowing, *"Without him, we can do nothing."*

Romans 6:
The 'set-free' Message

The following word is both a word of great hope as well as a strong warning against heresy.

According to the Bible Dictionary; the definition of **heresy** is as follows: *"The Scriptures is the standard of faith. Any opinion that is repugnant (contrary) to its doctrines is **heresy.**"*

In order to receive the glorious hope of having the power of sin destroyed in our lives; we must first warn against the heresy of those who teach something different than that taught especially in **Romans 6**. Paul warned Timothy in strong terms regarding false prophets and false teachers teaching contrary to the apostles' doctrine.

If I were to pick one passage of scripture out of the whole Bible relating to our being freed from sins' stranglehold it usurps on many believers; It would be **Romans 6**! I know we need the whole council of the Word of God. But right now, I'm just concentrating on this powerful message to the Church.

Concerning heresy; I will address it first. With God's help and through what the Word of God really teaches, I will expose this false doctrine and teaching which does not come from above; but is devilish, leading believers into a life of more sin, disobedience, and defeat in their lives.

I've heard and seen many sources from TV, on the radio, and from pulpits, those who teach and preach several misconceptions. One, is that our flesh is too weak and has dominion and authority over us. They say things like, *"It is impossible to live above sin and be overcomers!"* They say, *"We all sin every day in either words, deeds, or evil thoughts."* They say, *"We have no choices in the matter as to whether we give in to sin and whether we are disobedient or not."*

Romans 6 will clearly show that those ways of thinking, have their origins in men's opinions only–therefore a damnable heresy! Those who teach such falsehoods are blinded and cannot see afar off. They also fit into the category of those who *"Have a form of godliness; but deny the power thereof."* In their teachings, they deny the power in what **Jesus** did for us in paving the way for us to do it also (living godly overcoming lives).

Romans 6 (NLT):

In **verse 1**, we are asked a question, " ***Well then, should we keep on sinning so that God can show us more and more of his wonderful grace?"***

Verse 2 gives us the answer: *"Of course not! (God forbid in KJV) Since we have died to sin, how can we continue to live in it?"*

Verse 3 *"Or have you <u>forgotten</u> that when we were joined with Christ Jesus in baptism, we joined him in his death?"*

In other words, Paul is emphasizing the tendency for us to forget that we were joined with Christ in water baptism. Also as we go down under the water, it signifies death to self and death to the world. It is a stark reminder!

Verse 4 also explains what happens at baptism. *"For we died and were buried with Christ by baptism. And just as Christ was raised from the dead by the glorious power of the Father; now we also may live new lives."*

The possibility of living new overcoming lives is now made available. Praise the Lord!

Verse 5 *"Since we have been united with him in his death, we will also be raised to life as he was."*

Verse 6 *"We know that our old sinful selves were crucified with Christ so that sin might <u>lose its power</u> in our lives."*

It means that sin has lost its strength and authority over us. Our temptations may remain strong. Our flesh remains weak. But there is a way out now! There's a way of overcoming that which used to control and overcome us.

Verse 7 says, *"For when we died with Christ (buried in baptism), we were <u>set free from the power of sin.</u>"*

Notice the word 'power.' Sin itself was not destroyed, but its authority and dictatorship over us were destroyed (And that is accomplished only by faith).

Verse 8 "And since we died with Christ, we know also that we live with him."

We are buried with him in baptism and raised in a brand-new way of life.

Verse 9 *"We are sure of this because Christ was raised from the dead, and he will never die again. Death no longer has any power over him."*

Verse 10 *"When he died, he died once to <u>break the power of sin</u>. But now that he lives, <u>he lives for the glory of God.</u>"*

We too, can live to the glory of God because he did it first.

Verse 11 *"So you should also consider yourselves to be dead to the power of sin, and alive to God through Jesus Christ."*

We are to consider or deem it to be so–to be dead to sin's power but made alive through Jesus and the power of the Holy Spirit. If we don't consider or reckon it to be so; then we will remain under sin's power, authority, and dictatorship in our lives.

Verse 12 *"Do not let sin control the way you live, do not give in to sinful desires."*

Verse 13 *"Do not let any part of your body become an instrument of evil to serve sin. Instead, give yourselves completely to God, for <u>you were dead</u>, but now you have new life. So use your whole body as an instrument to do what is right for the glory of God."*

Verse 14 *"Sin is no longer your master, for you no longer live under the requirements of the law. Instead, you live under the freedom of God's grace."*

The laws of God are now written on our hearts and not on stone tablets. We now live under two great commandments: *"to love the Lord with all of our might.*

And to love our brother as ourselves." All of the commandments hinge on these two commands.

Verse 15 *"Well then, since God's grace has set us free from the law; does that mean we can go on sinning? Of course not!"*

Again, the sin question is asked and again, an emphatic answer is given! Then an explanation is given in **verse 16**. Grace does not give us freedom to keep on sinning as was the case before we were born again; but to set us free!

Verse 16 *"Don't you realize that you become the slaves of whatever you choose to obey? You can be a slave to sin, which leads to death, or you can choose to obey God, which leads to righteous living."*

Recognize, the word *'choose'*. We do have a choice in this matter! Also if we choose to obey God; it leads us into a Godly lifestyle. That is also what he desires for his children.

Verse 17 *"Thank God! You <u>were</u> slaves of sin, but now you wholeheartedly obey this teaching which we have given you."*

Notice the word <u>*'were'*</u>. It shouldn't be that way with us now! Notice the intensity of the word <u>*'wholeheartedly'*</u>. So many are half-hearted or lukewarm when it comes to their approach to living their lives for God! That's why their lives are miserable failures and poor examples of what Christians should exemplify and portray.

Verse 18 *"Now you are free from your slavery to sin, and you have become slaves to righteous living."*

How much clearer can it be made or portrayed than that? This verse speaks of victory! It does not have a tone of defeat in it whatsoever!

Verse 19 *"Because of the weakness of your human nature, I am using the illustration of slavery to help you understand all this. Previously you let yourselves be slaves to impurity and lawlessness, which led ever deeper into sin. Now you must give yourselves to be slaves to righteous living so that you will become holy."*

I'm afraid that many church-goers who claim to be followers of Jesus are still slaves to impurity and lawlessness which leads deeper into a life of sin—not away from it!

Verse 20-23 *"When you were slaves to sin, you were free from the obligation to do right. And what was the result? You are now ashamed of the things you used to do, things that end in eternal doom. But now you are free from the power of sin and have become slaves of God. Now you do those things that lead to holiness and result in eternal life. For the wages of sin is death, but the free gift of God is eternal life through Christ Jesus our Lord."*

We can never ever earn our way to heaven. We all have sinned and have come short of the Glory of God. We all deserve the penalty of death and banishment from the presence of our Lord. It's only through his great love, mercy, forgiveness, and grace that our salvation is made possible.

However, the Bible clearly teaches without holiness, we cannot see God! After salvation, God has expectations of us as his beloved children. The Lord has made a way for us to live abundantly, overcoming, victorious lives! Thank be to Jesus! What freedom!

It should be in every believer's heart to deeply desire to please and glorify Jesus. In obedience and striving through the power of the Holy Spirit, there exists the great possibilities presented in **Rom. 6,** which can help us mature in all that God has purposed for us to be!

Romans 6 gives great hope and encouragement in becoming more like our precious Lord and Savior Jesus Christ. Just to think that sin has lost its power over us! Recon, or deem it to be so! Then the victory, through Jesus, can be yours!

Wretched Man: Who Shall Deliver?

I believe one of the most misunderstood scripture passages is found in **Romans 7:14-24**. Many use this passage to declare Paul's wretchedness. They take that to explain that Paul was constantly being controlled by his fleshly nature. Nothing could be further from the truth! It was true previously, as he was living under the old covenant previous to his great revelation.

One of Paul's greatest revelations and solutions to man's sin problem came from his recognition of just how weak and wretched he was <u>if there was no solution</u> living under the old covenant (the old law). We experience his great dilemma too if there is no solution available to us.

In **Romans 7:14-24** Paul begins to see the problem as living under the old law, as left without a solution, *"For we know that the law is spiritual; but I am carnal sold under sin. For that which I do I allow not; for what I would, that do I not; but what I hate, that do I."*

Then Paul comes to a hopeless conclusion of who he was in **verse 24** *"Oh wretched man that I am!"* He understood that, though he wanted to do what was right, he was hopelessly bound to his carnal nature and was therefore a slave to unrighteousness and a slave to sin under the old law and without an answer to his helpless hopeless situation. We also need to have that same revelation. However, we need to see that God has a solution and answers. They can be found in **Rom. 6** and **Rom. 8**.

Paul asks a profound question as we should also ask. **Romans 7-24** *"Who shall deliver me from the body of this death?"*

'**Who**' is the key word in this verse. Paul was not left with a hopeless answer of, "Nobody!" He was not left answer-less. He was not left with, *"There is nobody that can help me out of my wretched condition!"*

Thanks be to God; Paul found the answer! And we can as well. The answer to Paul's question is found in **Romans 8:2-4**, It states, *"For the law of the Spirit of life in Christ Jesus hath made me free from the law of sin and death. For what the law could not do, in that it was weak, through the flesh, God sending his own Son in the likeness of sinful flesh, and for sin, condemned sin in the flesh; That the righteousness of the law might be fulfilled in us who walk not after the flesh, but after the Spirit."*

JESUS is the answer! Jesus condemned sin in the flesh as an answer and solution to the wretchedness problem that Paul spoke of because of the weakness of Paul's flesh (ours' as well).

Romans 6:14 clearly puts it so well, *"For sin shall not have dominion over you; for ye are not under the law, but under grace."* and in *verse 18* we read, *"Being then made free from sin, ye became the servants of righteousness."* The entire chapter of **Romans 6** speaks of victory! It speaks of our glorious deliverance from our wretched condition and bondage to sin, due to the weakness of our flesh.

I pray that all who read this chapter will study these scriptures over and over until they are deeply embedded in their hearts and minds. I pray that it will minister great encouragement and a new hope for God's children. My desire is that Holy Spirit revelation will come. I pray for an illumination to the reality that there is a high calling of victory and triumph in which the saints of God can attain and live in.

The Sin Problem and the Double Standard

Regarding the sin problem and how to deal with it in the Christian believer's walk: Many teachers and preachers hold onto a double standard. A double standard exists when we have a certain standard for others and a different one for our own lives.

Many teach and preach in such a way that even would suggest that Paul in the Bible had a double standard!

What do I mean by that? They teach that Paul was continually succumbing to his sinful nature. They misunderstand and misrepresent the verses in **Romans 7:14-24** where Paul is describing what he was like internally under the old law (covenant). He also was describing what it was and would be like without the Holy Spirit's power and workings in his life–attempting to keep the law with his own strength and willpower only. Rather than continuing on into **verse 25** and all of **Romans 8**; many stop at Paul's description of the things he would do—he doesn't. And the things he doesn't want to do; He does. Paul finishes by saying, *"Oh wretched man that I am."*

Their teachings and beliefs exist in such a way that they think Paul's whole life was taken up in defeat, sin, and wretchedness! That is ludicrous! How could he (Paul) have then gone on to say, *"Follow me, as I follow Christ."*

Several other scriptures speak of not only Paul but the other apostles as well were living as holy and godly examples for us to follow.

How could Paul have been living a defeated life of sinning consistently—and yet require a higher standard of deacons and elders?

Paul says in his letter to Timothy. In **1 Timothy 3:1-12** emphasizes that bishops (elders) and deacons must be found <u>blameless</u>. Then he gives several other requirements for the leaders of the Church to live victorious Godly lives.

Paul would have been setting one standard for himself, excusing himself for his wretchedness and fleshly weakness. And at the same time, giving these instructions, *"Hey, you fellas who desire to be elders or deacons, You must live at a higher standard than I do!"*

Thank God that Paul followed his own teachings and instructions!

Paul lived a God-fearing, overcoming life! Make no mistake about that! He lived by the same standards as the ones he laid out for deacons and elders.

We can point the finger at a pastor or evangelist who falls into the sin of adultery for example. Or we can have strong thoughts against a trouble-maker in the church. But we can excuse impatience, unkindness, harshness, bitterness, unforgiveness, and the like, in ourselves! That is living by a double-standard!

If we think that trouble-makers and adulterers have a choice in the matter; Then why do we excuse ourselves and others of our own sins by telling them, "We all sin everyday. And our flesh is weak. They will say, *"We have no choice because of our weakness! Therefore we will sin as long as we're living."* That thinking is grossly flawed!

There are numerous scriptures and Biblical promises on getting and maintaining victory over known sins and wickedness. In addition, scriptures are full of revelations and promises on how to accomplish that wonderful, liberating goal in our lives.

We often need a complete make-over and transformation in our way of thinking regarding the sin problem and how to deal with it. May God deliver us from double-mindedness and the double standards we cling to! Then the church as a whole, and we, as individual Christians, will be bright shining beacons of hope to one another and to the lost and hurting world!

Without that revelation, very little, if any change, growth, or transformation will take place in our inner beings. And we will truly be no different than the world!

Surviving the Storms

I was thinking of a tragedy that happened recently. A severe storm struck the Southern California coastal area. Many houses were demolished, as the ground beneath them gave way, causing them to break apart and tumble down the mostly—dirt and sand cliffs towards the sea below. These beautiful homes had tumbled down and crumbled because they were built on unstable ground. They were fine, as long as good conditions and peaceful weather conditions prevailed. But the softening of the soil by the torrential rains and the pounding of the violent surf took its toll. The powerful storm clearly exposed the weakness of the choice of those building sites and the type of ground on which they were built.

This same scenario can play out in our daily lives in the spiritual realm. In **Matt. 7:24-27** Jesus likens a wise man as to <u>one who heard his sayings, and then did them</u>; as to a man who built his house upon a rock. When the rains and floods and winds of hard times came; that wise man's house withstood the storms. He withstood under the pressures of life, the persecutions, the temptations, and the trials. Jesus teachings and his Word with the Holy Spirit's power and guidance cause the wise man to stand, being built upon solid rock!

James 1:22 says almost the same thought. *"But, be ye doers of the word, and not hearers only, deceiving your own selves."*

Those who believe they need only to hear the word without doing, are like what Jesus described about those who do not do his sayings; therefore their houses are built upon sand. When times get tough; when the trials of testings come; when hardships arrive; *"Great will be the fall of that house (that man)."* just like Jesus predicted. We will not spiritually survive if we don't take heed to his warning!

James 1:21 is an exhortation to help prepare us for what lies ahead; thereby giving us specific instructions on keeping us stable in life's storms.

James said, (NLT) ***"So get rid of all the filth and evil in your lives, and humbly accept the word God has planted in your hearts, for it has the power to save your souls."*** This verse is a prelude to being doers and not hearers only.

If we are wise by ***reading***, ***listening***, and ***doing*** God's Word; We will be planning and building well and on the right type of ground; substance that is stable and will withstand whatever life throws at us. We will be survivors! We will be more than conquerors! We will not become victims of disaster and shipwreck in our spiritual walks with Jesus.

Spirit of Truth and Spirit of Error

I've often wondered how some believers, teachers, and preachers can be in harmony with God, his Word, and his truth; while others are deceived and misled. In addition, they often lead others astray into the wrong way! Their beliefs are in those ideas and theologies that truly are contrary to a holy mighty God and His holy Word.

Why does deception happen? How does it come about? What is to prevent you and I from being deceived and led ourselves astray?

There are no simple and easy answers to these tough questions. But I will attempt, with the Lord's help, to explain just a few:

One reason is there exists a lack of deep hunger and thirst after righteousness, which is a foundational and vital ingredient needed by every child of God. The Word says that **"If you hunger and thirst after righteousness, You shall be filled."** No hunger—no filling! Simple as that! Error and deception are the results!

Another reason professing brothers and sisters are easily led astray is that they love their disobedient behavior! They look for any excuses or loopholes they can, in the scriptures, to justify and strengthen themselves in their sins. Accountability and personal responsibility will cost them. And that hurts the flesh! There is no experience of the fear of God! There is also a lack of desire concerning following Christ and his commands, that being to do those things that are pleasing in his sight. Their whole understanding of the Bible is warped and affected by this thinking. The Bible says, *"**They are blind and cannot see afar off**, and have forgotten that they were purged (cleansed) from their old sins."*

Another reason for deception and misunderstanding of scriptures is that many start backwards from the complicated to the simple; rather than from the simple to the more hard-to-understand scriptures in the Bible. They start out trying to understand the meat of the Word, before understanding the milk of the Word.

As an analogy: Instead of starting out with basic math—they start with Algebra or Trigonometry—then work backwards in trying to explain and understand the basics. Unless you start out and understand that **1+1=2** and get that down as fundamental and foundational, how will you understand properly and put into use the knowledge of: **c=d squared divided by the square root of L + R to the 7th power?**

Since they think they understand this equation properly when in reality, they really don't, They then go back to the basics and try to explain away, add to, or take away from the basic fact that **1+1=2**. They actually attempt to convey that 1+1 really **does not equal 2**! This way of learning and teaching also happens when attempting to explain the things of God, leading to deception.

Peter explains what happens when we don't really understand and yet believe and teach from those misunderstandings some of the more complicated things of God's words and ways. Peter speaks concerning Paul, his brother and co-laborer in the faith, in **2 Peter 3:15-17** when he states: **(NLT)** *"Paul also wrote to you with the wisdom of God gave him, speaking of these things in all of his letters. Some of his comments are hard to understand, and those who are ignorant and unstable have twisted his letters to mean something quite different just as they do with other parts of Scripture. And will result in their destruction. You already know these things, dear friends. So be on guard; then you will not be carried away by the errors of these wicked people and lose your own secure footing."*

A good example of what I'm saying is this: Many try to understand and explain Paul's teachings concerning the sovereignty of God, predestination, and security in Christ. They start with these harder-to-be-understood teachings, and without really understanding these true principles in their proper perspectives and totality of scriptures; They then go back to the basic principles of the Word, and contradict and twist these very easy basic clear words, in justifications of their inaccurate beliefs. Sometimes they even reject these very basic principles and fundamentals altogether!

On the very easy-to-understand teachings in the gospel in regards to living victoriously as overcomers for Jesus; It is completely refuted and rejected as heresy by these misled folks. When in fact; The scriptures speak much concerning victory, how to obtain it, and practical application in daily living triumphantly for Jesus.

These scriptures on overcoming sin are obvious and are basic pure undefiled milk of the Word—and are found throughout the scriptures. The basic fundamentals can be understood even by the newborn baby Christian. *"God has hidden these things from the wise and prudent, and has revealed them unto babes,"* the Bible states.

Because of some professing Christians skewed beliefs and misunderstandings, there is a rejection and explaining away all of **Romans 6 and 8**. When they try to explain **Romans 7**, they mistakenly slander Paul by giving the impression that he was a slave to his flesh and carnal nature, that his flesh was too weak. While it is true that Paul recognized how weak his flesh was. He realized that there was hope and resurrection power in God and the Holy Spirit available to him in overcoming those weaknesses! He explains this very clearly and thoroughly in **chapter 6** and **chapter 8** of **Romans**.

Many who believe there is no victory believe that Jesus life and death were for salvation only. They believe that Jesus' life and death had nothing to do with what was accomplished by the defeating of sin in his human body. There is little understanding that Christ's life and death on the cross was for the purpose of destroying the power of sin and it's slavery and authority over the believers. It was not only for the salvation of our souls. They do not really have faith that if we totally depend and rely on the Holy Spirit for our source of power and strength; that we can overcome any sin!

Why would Paul have lived a hypocritical life by teaching **Romans 6** on the one hand; while not practicing what he preached? How could we follow Paul as he followed Christ, if indeed he was walking a defeated unholy life and was enslaved to sin, or that he was harboring secret sins?

That portion of **Romans 7** where Paul speaks of the weakness of his flesh, is misunderstood, misrepresented by many teachers, and turned into something that absolutely contradicts and refutes all of Paul's own teachings! These teachers and preachers say that it is impossible to live victoriously over sin. They teach, contrary to scriptures that we will always remain in bondage to our sinful natures. And therefore, we have no opportunity or choice in the matter of battling sin in the Spirit and winning. There is a rebelling against the thought that we can be more than conquerors through Christ Jesus who strengthens us, concerning overcoming wickedness and evil in our lives.

Romans 6 is basic, leaving no misunderstanding whatsoever on God's will, purposes, and possibilities. If only there could be true faith exercised by God's people, in these scriptures! The light would then shine out of darkness, thus dispelling the deception!

Why would God provide all that we need to live a Godly life? Why would he supply us mighty spiritual weapons and how to use them, if they were never-the-less useless and ineffective?

Why do Christians put these spiritual weapons and armor in a locked-up weapons cabinet? Could the reason be because they think these weapons and armor will do them no good anyways?

One of the ways of protecting ourselves from misunderstanding scriptures and being deceived is to realize that it can happen to anyone including ourselves. It takes a real hunger for all of God. It takes admitting when we have been deceived. That is a very difficult and humbling thing to do.

There comes a time for the need of many believers, to go back and desire the sincere milk of the Word starting with the basics.

Many years ago, in my own life's experience, I realized I was believing and living in spiritual deception. It was a needed and very humbling experience for me to let go of those wrong beliefs and start all over with the basics. It was one of the most difficult and humbling things I have experienced in my Christian walk. But it became a starting place for me, and a progression from there to the more complex things of God. I told the Lord that I was willing to forget everything I ever was taught, everything I believed in and held dear; all except that I knew that Jesus died for my sins, and that I had a born-again experience. That's about as basic of a beginning place that one can start from!

Once I did that; I hungered for truth and nothing but truth; having no desire whatsoever to take the liberty of changing God's holy Word in any way. He has been faithful in revealing to me the errors in my past beliefs and interpretations, I began a journey of the Lord undoing that which was not of him. He also gave back and reconfirmed the precious truth that I had been taught and learned through the scriptures! As the saying goes, *"You don't throw the baby out with the bath water!"* I'm still a work in progress. I still am learning. And maybe there are a few things I must still unlearn and see from Jesus perspective. That's where true humility must come into play and remain as part of the believer's ongoing life in the Lord. *"God resists the proud, but gives grace unto the humble."*

The Bible says, *"Let God be truth; and every man a liar."* His ways are not our ways. Let us only be interested in his instructions, teachings, and insights. May we be like the Bereans and check everything we're taught by the Word of God as authority and source of truth. May our own thoughts be dismantled and cast away.

When we have that knowledge and attitude; We are well on our way to being protected from heresy, deception, and false teaching. Then we have the beautiful possibility to grow in the Lord and to be transformed into His image day by day.

Let us be a lover of God's Word. May we treat it with all due respect with Godly fear. Let it be our only reliable and dependable source of spiritual life, truth, and guidance!

Like a Roaring Lion

How easy it is for us Christians to be taken off-guard and surprised by Satan. Instead of being prepared in our minds in advance; We are caught quickly off-guard before we even realize what is happening.

Many times we give in to our carnal natures by reacting spontaneously during temptations and attacks by our enemy. Afterward, the Holy Spirit faithfully comes on the scene. He convicts us into asking God's and sometimes people's forgiveness as well.

It is wonderful that we have the much-needed forgiveness and mercy of God. <u>But our walk in Christ should be more than that!</u> There's a high calling in Christ Jesus. The high calling is for us to get victory over our flesh and the enemy of our soul, the devil. It not only is commanded in the Scriptures; It is possible!

A scripture comes to mind, with powerful exhortation regarding a call to alertness and keen awareness of life's situations and dangers.

I Peter 5:8 & **9 KJV** says, *"Be sober, be vigilant; because your adversary the devil, as a roaring lion, walketh about seeking whom he may devour. Whom resist steadfast in the faith, knowing that the same afflictions are accomplished in your brethren that are in the world."* The **NLT** puts it this way: <u>*"Stay alert."*</u> and <u>*"Watch out!"*</u>

The Bible gives very specific instructions for us, in regard to being on the utmost lookout at all times. The devil acts just like a lion does. He uses very similar tactics. He is sneaky. He is wily. He creeps up on his prey quietly at times. Other times, he roars, sending paralyzing fear directed at his surprised victims. For the prey; (that's us) The short lapse in response time and the momentary inactivity on our part gives our predator, the devil, the time needed to carry out his attack to its violent conclusion.

He pounces suddenly on the sleeping ones! The casual brothers and sisters become his easy targets. At times those sick in body, in their weakened conditions, are singled out. Children of God who are sick in their spiritual life and walk with the Lord, are very vulnerable. Finally, those who are mentally worn out and tired, become primary targets also. Those who are distracted by other things and cares of life and those who become separated from the flock are singled out because of their vulnerability. The devil wanders about, looking for these easy ones to pick off.

We can make it difficult or easy for him. He will attack all of us. But the question is, "Are we ready for it?"

Wouldn't it really be stupid for us not to be on the alert in the following situations:

You are in grizzly bear country and paying no attention at all to the potential danger all around you! Or you are walking across the Serengeti in Africa, all alone and without a weapon, and not paying attention! Your mind is on other things and not on the dangers at hand! Yet that's how many are living out their daily Christian lives in that very dangerous way?

The devil also attacks the healthy and wise ones probing for possible weaknesses. But his job becomes much more difficult. Not only are the wise and healthy alert ones found amongst the protection of the herd (brothers and sisters in the Lord); But they run for protection to their unbeatable mighty shepherd and Lord!

Those who put their trust in the Lord and call out for his help–those who are alert–those who remain in the safety of fellowship–do not become easy prey–thereby being caught unaware and off-guard by Satan's sly tactics!

While on the alert and during times of stress and sudden attack from our enemy–Saying the kind word–doing the good deed–reacting in the right way–becomes much more doable and obtainable. That is only made possible as we have our focus on being wide awake and aware of our circumstances. In times of temptations and satanic attacks, we are only protected as we rely on the Holy Spirit to send up the alert signals. Those warnings call out to us, ***"Watch out! There's an enemy on the prowl!"***

Part of our success is in knowing our own personal tendencies and weaknesses. Those will be the devil's primary target areas.

Only as we are in the state of awareness and being privy to the devil's tactics is the possibility for us to react in the right way and to do and speak that which is right and God-pleasing.

Above all, we must put our complete trust and faith in the Lord. With his help and his provided spiritual weapons, we can defeat Satan when we are under his ambushing tactics and attacks. With weapons in hand and alertness our way of life; The devil's roars and his growls will only be that of a toothless old lion! Our God is infinitely greater than he! And it is He who is in us and for us. He will give us the victory!

The Measure of Success or Failure is Love

There's a 60's song, whose lyrics go something like this, *"What the world needs now–is love–sweet love."* It also continues, *"There's just–too little of."*

The Bible says, **"In the last days, the love for many will wax cold."**

OUR GREATEST PRIORITY AND MEASURE OF SUCCESS IS TO LOVE.

Matt. 22:37-40 The two greatest commandments are these: *"Thou shalt love the Lord thy God with all thy heart, and with all thy soul, and with all thy mind. This is the first and great commandment. And the second is like unto it, thou shalt love thy neighbor as thyself. On these two commandments hang all the law and the prophets."*

"To love God." "To love man." Both are interconnected, intertwined, and linked together and cannot be separated in God's view.

Phil. 2:1-4 *"Let nothing be done out of selfishness."* and *"Consider others better than self."*

The Early church had a burning love for God and one another. They sold all that they had and gave to one another. It was not necessarily wisdom as they were later instructed to occupy. But it was a tremendous show of unselfish love for one another!

It is impossible to love God without loving our fellowman.

God takes it very personal concerning the love or lack thereof and how we treat others!

Matt. 25:33-45 *"Such as ye have done unto others----ye have done unto me."*

Love is far more than just a fuzzy feeling or merely saying, "I love you!" it could cost us something. Read **I Cor. 13.**

The Word of God says we are to*, "Offer our bodies a living sacrifice."* I believe this is speaking not only about our sacrifice unto God; but as we sacrificially show our love in good deeds to the benefit others.

Regarding our ministry to the church: It is of vital importance to be motivated from a heart of compassion and love. It must not be motivated out of selfish ambitions, pride, or recognition.

Important questions to ask ourselves:

"What can I do to encourage and edify others? What can I do to help others? How can I help carry someone's heavy burden and load?

To love God and to Love Man is our primary purpose in this life. It we fail in those areas—THEN OUR WHOLE LIVES WILL HAVE BEEN DISASTOROUS FAILURES!

If loving God and loving our fellow man has been our top priorities; WE WILL HAVE BEEN A SUCCESS IN LIFE'S JOURNEY!

The great challenge to all Christians:

Dare to step out of our comfort zones

Dare to strive for the high calling in Christ!

Dare to be overcomers!

Dare to fly!